Raptor World

Falcons

by Jenna Lee Gleisner

Bullfrog Books

Ideas for Parents and Teachers

Bullfrog Books let children practice reading informational text at the earliest reading levels. Repetition, familiar words, and photo labels support early readers.

Before Reading

- Discuss the cover photo. What does it tell them?
- Look at the picture glossary together. Read and discuss the words.

Read the Book

- "Walk" through the book and look at the photos. Let the child ask questions. Point out the photo labels.
- Read the book to the child, or have him or her read independently.

After Reading

- Prompt the child to think more. Ask: Peregrine falcons are the fastest birds in the world! What other animals do you know of that are fast? Do they fly, run, or swim?

Bullfrog Books are published by Jump!
5357 Penn Avenue South
Minneapolis, MN 55419
www.jumplibrary.com

Library of Congress Cataloging-in-Publication Data

Names: Gleisner, Jenna Lee, author.
Title: Falcons / by Jenna Lee Gleisner.
Description: Bullfrog books edition.
Minneapolis, MN : Jump!, Inc., [2020]
Series: Raptor World
Audience: Age 5-8. | Audience: K to Grade 3.
Includes index.
Identifiers: LCCN 2018038340 (print)
LCCN 2018039068 (ebook)
ISBN 9781641286299 (ebook)
ISBN 9781641286282 (hardcover : alk. paper)
ISBN 9781641288217 (pbk.)
Subjects: LCSH: Falcons—Juvenile literature.
Classification: LCC QL696.F34 (ebook)
LCC QL696.F34 G59 2020 (print)
DDC 598.9/6—dc23
LC record available at https://lccn.loc.gov/2018038340

Editor: Susanne Bushman
Designer: Jenna Casura

Photo Credits: Harald Schmidt/iStock, cover; Kaphoto/iStock, 1; Ondrej Prosicky/Shutterstock, 3; Ali Bernie Buga-ay/Shutterstock, 4; jnara/iStock, 5; NaturePL/Superstock, 6–7; Nature Picture Library/Alamy, 8–9, 23bl; Ian Duffield/Shutterstock, 10–11, 23br; Mark Medcalf/Shutterstock, 12; Eric Isselee/Shutterstock, 13; Thomas Harbig/Minden Pictures/Superstock, 14–15; Mike Mulick/Shutterstock, 16–17, 23tr; John Gooday/Alamy, 18; Independent birds/Shutterstock, 19; imageBROKER/Superstock, 20–21, 23tl; Red ivory/Shutterstock, 22; barbaraaaa/iStock, 24.

Printed in the United States of America at Corporate Graphics in North Mankato, Minnesota.

Table of Contents

Fast Fliers

Zoom!

What is that bird?

A falcon!

There are at least 40 kinds.

The peregrine is one.

It is the fastest animal in the world!

How fast?

As fast as a race car!

Wow!

It hunts prey in the air!

Falcons have great vision.

It helps them hunt.

Nice!

Some hunt with talons.
They dig in.

Others use their beaks. They are sharp!

Rip!

This one eats.

It tears off chunks.

Yum!

perch

It rests.

On what?

A perch.

It looks.

For what?

Prey that runs.

Lizards. Mice.

Prey that flies.
Birds. Bats.

It feeds its chicks. They will grow up. They will hunt, too!

chick

Built to Hunt

wings
Falcons have pointed wings. They fold them in close to their bodies when they dive.

feathers
Falcon feathers are dense and tightly packed. Not much air can get through them while the falcon flies. This helps it fly faster.

beak
The beak is hooked and sharp. This helps the falcon tear and eat prey. Some falcons use their beaks to kill their prey.

talons
Sharp talons help falcons catch, carry, and kill prey.

Picture Glossary

chicks
Baby birds.

perch
A raised place where something sits.

prey
Animals that are hunted by other animals for food.

vision
The sense of sight.

Index

To Learn More

Finding more information is as easy as 1, 2, 3.

1. Go to www.factsurfer.com
2. Enter "falcons" into the search box.
3. Click the "Surf" button to see a list of websites.